LOA
GRADUATES

31 Devotions
To Revolutionize Your Future

A Devotional by
Kenneth and Gloria Copeland

HARRISON HOUSE
Tulsa, Oklahoma

08 07 06 05 04   10 9 8 7 6 5 4 3 2 1

Load Up for Graduates:
31 Devotions To Revolutionize Your Future
ISBN 1-57794-651-0   KC-21-0018
Copyright © 2004 by Kenneth and Gloria Copeland
Kenneth Copeland Ministries
Fort Worth, Texas 76192-0001

Published by Harrison House, Inc.
P.O. Box 35035
Tulsa, Oklahoma 74153

The Future is Yours

You are the future. What you do with your life determines the future. You are only one person, but God can take one person and change nations. In the prophetic age that we live, He is looking for nation changers. That may sound unreal, but with God it is absolutely a possibility.

The bottom line is that your destiny as a Christian is to grow up in Jesus. Eternity is in the balance—the eternal lives of hundreds, possibly thousands or hundreds of thousands, depend on you fulfilling your part of God's plan. But to do it your own way is to fail. If you are truly to succeed in this life and bring glory to God, you have to do it God's way. You have to seek His guidance through His Word and through taking time to talk with the Holy Spirit. He can't guide you unless you are talking to Him and listening to Him speak to your spirit—that's what prayer is. The devotions you are about to read will help you develop this relationship with God and take hold of your future.

—*Kenneth and Gloria Copeland*

Your Load Up Instructions

1. Start each devotion by reading the Scripture verse at the top of the page. Ask yourself what God is saying and allow the Holy Spirit to speak to you.

2. Read the devotion. Then take a moment to think about what you read and how it applies to your life today. You can write notes directly on the page if you want.

3. Read the passages marked *Backup* at the bottom of the page. These "extra bytes" will help you get the most out of each devotion.

4. Put action behind what you have just read by speaking the *Voice Activate*. Speak it in faith and meditate on it all day long!

That's it! Enjoy your new *Load Up* devotional. Use it to its fullest and receive all that God has for you!

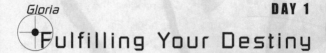

Gloria

DAY 1

Fulfilling Your Destiny

> "As you sent me into the world, I have
> sent them into the world."
> —John 17:18

"What's God's plan for my life?" We've all
asked that question at some time or another.
We're all eager to fulfill the divine purpose for our
lives, but we need direction in finding out what
that plan is.

The truth is, God never intended for us to be
in the dark about His plan for us. He left us clear,
written instructions. What's more, He gave us a
pattern to follow so we could see how to carry
out those instructions.

The pattern is Jesus. Our call is to continue
His ministry. I know that sounds like a tall order,
but it's true. Jesus said so in John 17:18.

Once we realize Jesus is the pattern, we
need to find out exactly what Jesus was sent to
do. Well, the Bible's pretty clear: "The reason the

Son of God appeared was to destroy the devil's work" (1 John 3:8).

Think about that. You're called to finish what Jesus began: to destroy Satan's work on the earth. That is the job God wants us to do, and we do it the same way Jesus did. After all, He promised, "Anyone who has faith in me will do what I have been doing. He will do even greater things than these, because I am going to the Father" (John 14:12).

In short, Jesus' ministry was comprised of three functions: 1) He healed the sick, 2) He cast out demons, and 3) He preached the good news.

Now, I know it's easy to do the preaching and not the other two works. However, the Bible was never designed to be preached without proof that Jesus is alive today. Jesus didn't just say, "God loves you." He demonstrated it. He proved the truth of what He was saying by operating in the supernatural power of God.

He expects us to do the same. That's God's plan for your life!

b a c k u p

Matthew 8:16, 9:35

v o i c e   a c t i v a t e

I believe in Jesus. I am sent

by Him. I fulfill God's plan

for my life. John 17:18

God 24/7

"Do not let your hearts be troubled."
—John 14:1

People everywhere—including Christians—run around pulling their hair out, worrying about what to do, but there's no need to panic. After all, Jesus told us what to do. He said, "Do not let your hearts be troubled."

When Jesus said those words to His disciples, they were about to face more trouble than most of us can imagine. Jesus was about to be crucified before their eyes. Peter was about to deny Him. Who can even imagine how stressful those days must have been?

Yet Jesus said to them, "Do not let your hearts be troubled."

He went on to teach how to have an untroubled heart even in the most troubling times.

He said, "Remain in me, and I will remain in you. No branch can bear fruit by itself; it must remain in the vine. Neither can you bear fruit unless you remain in me. I am the vine; you are the branches.... If you remain in me and my words remain in you, ask whatever you wish, and it will be given you. This is to my Father's glory, that you bear much fruit..." (John 15:4-5, 7-8).

When you remain in Jesus, He's not just God on Sundays. He's not just the One you think about when you get in trouble or have a hard test. No, when you remain in Him, He's God from Monday through Sunday. He's involved in your life 24/7.

Remain in Jesus by talking to Him throughout the day and remembering His Word to you. For if His Word remains in you, it will constantly teach you God's ways and wisdom. His promises will keep your heart from being troubled!

b a c k u p
Proverbs 8:10-17

v o i c e   a c t i v a t e
I do not let my heart be

troubled because I trust and

remain in Jesus. John 14:1

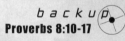

Living the Good Life

> "For we are God's [own] handiwork (His workmanship), recreated in Christ Jesus, [born anew] that we may do those good works which God predestined (planned beforehand) for us, [taking paths which He prepared ahead of time] that we should walk in them—living the good life which He prearranged and made ready for us to live."
>
> —Ephesians 2:10, AMP

Every day it touches me how good God is to us. You and I are God's favorites! I know we are because God's mercy and favor are over all His works (Psalm 145:9)—and Ephesians 2:10 says we are all His workmanship!

Psalm 145:8-9 says, "The Lord is gracious and compassionate, slow to anger and rich in love. The Lord is good to all; he has compassion on all he has made."

God is gracious. Do you know what that means? It means He is inclined to show favors.

It's just His nature to bless people. He is also compassionate. The word *compassion* doesn't just mean He has pity on us. It means "eager yearning."

Isn't that wonderful? God is eagerly yearning to do you good! In fact, the Bible says He is looking for someone to bless. He is not satisfied unless He can do someone good (2 Chronicles 16:9).

I remember the day I realized that. I was desperate for help. I picked up the Bible and read in Matthew 6:26 that God cared for the birds of the air. What an amazing thought that was to me! No one had ever told me God was good. They had never told me He loved me. They just told me a lot of "do nots."

When I read that scripture, I thought, *Well, if God cares for birds, surely He cares for me!* I gave God my life and asked Him to do something with it, and that's all it took. I gave God an opening and His love flooded through it.

God wants to do you good. He wants you to live the good life! So, the next time someone tells you God wants you to be sick or downtrodden, just remember that God has a good life planned for you, even in this dark world. A life of health. A life of joy. A life of ministering to and helping people. That good life has been set up for you and made ready for you to live. Everything you need—a family, friends, a home, a good job, a future mate—it has all been stored up with your name on it. So go for it! Receive your destiny! Live the good life!

backup
Matthew 6:25-34

voice activate
I live the good life which God has prearranged and made ready for me to live. Ephesians 2:10, AMP

Kenneth   **DAY 4**

Get Ready for Power

> **"I can do all things through Christ [the Anointed One and His Anointing] which strengtheneth me."**
>
> **—Philippians 4:13, KJV**

Notice in today's verse Paul didn't say, "I can do all things through Christ who strengtheneth me."

He said, "which strengtheneth me."

He wasn't just talking about Christ, the Anointed One of God. He was also talking about the abilities He has—or, the anointing!

As a Christian, God has provided you with the ability to do everything He has called you to do—no matter how great or how small the task. He has given to you His power. That power is the anointing that is inside you, ready to empower you to do whatever God has called you to do.

When you understand that, it will change the way you read and understand the instructions God has given us about how we're to live.

In Ephesians 4, for example, Paul says, "Walk worthy of the vocation wherewith ye are called...Endeavoring to keep the unity of the Spirit...sin not...Let no corrupt communication proceed out of your mouth...grieve not the holy Spirit of God...be ye kind one to another, tenderhearted, forgiving one another, even as God for Christ's sake hath forgiven you" (verses 1, 3, 26, 29-30, 32, KJV).

Why is it so important that we follow these instructions from Paul? He says it's for Christ's sake. It's for the sake of the anointing – the power He has given you to accomplish His will! In other words, it's our job to keep ourselves in a place where God can anoint us with His power, so we can bring Jesus' love to those around us.

When you realize that, you'll begin to protect that anointing and not allow anything to hinder the power of God inside you.

b a c k u p
Ephesians 4:26-32

v o i c e   a c t i v a t e
I can do all things through the

Anointed One and His Anointing

which strengthens me!

Philippians 4:13

Choosing To Be Different

"Do not be so deceived and misled! Evil companionships (communion, associations) corrupt and deprave good manners and morals and character."

—1 Corinthians 15:33, AMP

A lot of people don't understand Christians. They say we are unusual and have no fun. They don't understand that we do the things we do simply because we love God—and because God says it is right. They don't understand how rewarding living for God is. We have good health, wealth, godly friendships, things working right at home and at work. People in the world don't feel like they have anything in common with you. They've never experienced God's peace.

First Corinthians 15:33 tells you that you'll be influenced to do wrong if you stay friends with wrongdoers. Now that you're a Christian, you shouldn't want to hang out in the same places you once did. You're living a new life.

Later on, as you grow stronger, you might be able to be around some of that old stuff without temptation. However, you have to be very careful until you learn how to walk completely free of your old lifestyle. Many times you have to break off old friendships. You have to listen to God about where you're to go and whom you're to hang around. You can love your old friends and people in the world, but you can't spend time with them in the same way you once did.

You know the way to peace. You know the right way to live. You know in your heart where you should spend your time, and the places you need to avoid. So follow your heart. It doesn't matter that no one understands. It's okay to be called strange or different—especially when you're full of God's peace.

backup
2 Corinthians 6:14-18

voice activate

I refuse to be deceived or misled by having evil associations or companions. I choose to fellowship with those who believe in the Lord Jesus Christ.

1 Corinthians 15:33, AMP

Kenneth

Forgive–Period

> "And when you stand praying, if you hold anything against anyone, forgive him, so that your Father in heaven may forgive you your sins."
>
> —Mark 11:25-26

Unforgiveness is downright dangerous. It will make your spirit weak and your prayers ineffective. It will pull the plug on your faith so much so that you won't have enough power to effectively live as a Christian.

In Mark 11, Jesus didn't say, "When you stand praying, try to forgive," or "When you stand praying, forgive if you can." He simply said, "Forgive." Period.

Jesus made forgiveness a command. It wouldn't be right for Him to command us to do something we couldn't do. So you can be sure it's within your power to obey His command and forgive—no matter how badly you've been hurt.

Most people don't realize it, but unforgiveness is actually a form of fear. Quite often we don't forgive because we're afraid of getting hurt again. We're afraid we're never going to recover from the damage that person has done to us.

If you want to forgive, get rid of those fears. How? By filling your mind and heart with God's promises that apply to your situation (Psalm 119:11).

If you'll do that, I can assure you, your feelings will change. It may not happen overnight...but it will happen. One of these days, almost without thinking, you'll throw your arms around that person, give them a big hug, and say, "I love you, friend." What's more, you'll mean it from the bottom of your heart.

backup
Luke 6:27-36, 17:3-4

voice activate
I forgive those I have anything against so God can forgive my sins. Mark 11:25-26

Gloria

A Firewall of Favor

> "For surely, O Lord, you bless the
> righteous; you surround them with your
> favor as with a shield."
> —Psalm 5:12

It doesn't matter what kind of trouble you
may find yourself in. God's favor is always strong
enough to get you out! All you have to do is tap
into it...by faith.

If you want to enjoy God's favor in your life,
start believing it's there. Get into the Bible. Put
His promises into your heart and speak them
aloud. Begin to believe what God's Word says
and act on it.

If you'll do that, you won't be defeated in
any area of your life. Because there is no
situation, no circumstance, no disaster—nothing
Satan has ever done or can do—that is stronger
than God's favor.

The Apostle Paul proved that. He faced more
trouble than most of us could ever imagine. He

gives a list of the things that happened to him in 2 Corinthians 11:23-29—beatings, stonings, jail, shipwrecks.

Paul said those things came to him because an evil spirit had been sent to stop him. This evil spirit came to stop him from preaching the truth. Paul called the spirit "a thorn in my flesh" (2 Corinthians 12:7).

That demon worked hard to shut Paul's mouth and throw him off course, but nothing worked. Why? God's favor was with Paul.

Remember that when troubles come against you. When Satan is trying to mess up your life and it looks like there's absolutely no way out of a problem, don't lose hope. God's power comes through in those situations. His favor is always enough to bring you out on top.

So speak to that trouble you're facing today. Say: "I'm a child of God and I know the Bible says His favor surrounds me like a shield. It can easily pull me out of this trouble. So I put my faith in this promise from God to me. I believe His

favor is surrounding me and I'm coming out of
this a winner!"

b a c k u p
Acts 7:8-10

v o i c e   a c t i v a t e

The Lord blesses me because

I am righteous. He surrounds

me with His favor like a shield.

Psalm 5:12

Dreaming Beyond the Possible

"You will be blessed when you come in and blessed when you go out."
—Deuteronomy 28:6

People always talk about one day building their "dream home." Did you know that you can build dreams out of God's Word? Oh, yeah! A good foundation for them is Deuteronomy 28. I can tell you from experience, the truth found here is good dream-building material.

God intended for us to be dreamers. He made us that way. He didn't intend for us to be limited by the things around us. He meant for us to dream beyond them. He meant for us to dream about doing things—today and tomorrow—that are far beyond what naturally seems possible.

That's what Abraham did. He locked into God's dream—and it was bigger than anything he could have thought up on his own.

It will be that way for you, too. God's dream is bigger than your dream for yourself. It is way more than you could ask for or even think up! (Ephesians 3:20).

Once you get that dream inside you, things will begin to change. No, all your problems won't disappear overnight. But you'll react to them differently.

When trouble rises up in front of you and threatens to defeat you, God's dream will stir in your heart.

You'll start saying, "Wait just a minute. I'm on top of this thing, not stuck underneath. I don't have to put up with this situation. I happen to be a child of God! No weapon used against me can defeat me!" (See Deuteronomy 28:13 and Isaiah 54:17.)

Building your dream home is great...but building God's dreams inside of you, and then seeing those dreams come to pass, is even better.

backup
Psalm 23

voice activate
I am blessed when I come in

and blessed when I go out.

Deuteronomy 28:6

Gloria

The Greater One Lives in You!

> **"For we are members of His body, of His flesh and of His bones."**
> **—Ephesians 5:30, NKJV**

Today, if anyone is going to see Jesus, they'll have to see Him through Christians. We're His physical Body! If His Body doesn't preach the good news, the good news doesn't get preached. If His Body doesn't reach out to the hurting, then His ministry to them is cut short.

That thought surprises some people. They think Jesus changed somehow after He rose again and went to heaven. They think He stopped being interested in ministering personally to people like He did when He was on earth, but Jesus didn't change. He is the same yesterday, today, and forever (Hebrews 13:8). He still wants to preach the good news to people. He still wants to cast out demons and heal the sick. He still has the power to do all those things—and even more! (John 14:12).

How does He get them done? Through you and me.

Point your finger at yourself right now and say out loud, "I am the Body of Jesus. He is living in me right now!"

When that truth comes alive in you, impossible tasks won't overwhelm you anymore. You won't give up, because you'll know that God is in you, and He has the power to get the job done. When He calls you to preach and you can't talk very well, you'll just say, "Well, that's all right. Jesus is in me and He'll give me the words." When someone who's sick comes to you for prayer, you won't want to bolt and run. You'll be eager to pray for that person because you'll know the Healer lives in you.

The Greater One lives in you! Now believe it! Live like it!

backup
1 John 4:1-6

voice activate

The One Who is in me is

greater than the one who

is in the world! 1 John 4:4

Not Guilty

> "So Jesus is not ashamed to call them [us] brothers."
> —Hebrews 2:11

All of us struggle with bad habits at some time or another. We work hard to change them. There may be some things in your life today where it's a little hard to get control. You may have to resist Satan in those areas. You can take God's Word and put him out of commission.

In the meantime, do not allow yourself to be harassed by him or made to feel guilty. It's dangerous.

Don't let yourself or anyone else say things like, "I'm so messed up. I'm so bad. I'm so worthless." That's directly opposite of what God says. If Jesus walked through the door and stood right there for the next 20 years talking every minute of every day, He would never call you worthless. It's proven in Hebrews 2.

Jesus is not ashamed of you. Therefore, you don't have any business being ashamed of yourself!

Start believing what the Bible says. Believe that you're God's special workmanship, created in Jesus. Start saying that. Instead of talking about what a messed-up person you are, start agreeing with what God says and know that you are in right-standing with God (2 Corinthians 5:21). Practice seeing yourself that way. Practice seeing yourself without those bad habits. After all, Jesus has already beaten them for you. So believe it today by faith!

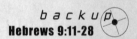

b a c k u p
Hebrews 9:11-28

v o i c e   a c t i v a t e
Jesus is not ashamed of me;

therefore, I am not ashamed.

Hebrews 2:11

Overloaded
With His Spirit

> **"If anyone does not remain in me, he
> is like a branch that is thrown away
> and withers."**
> **—John 15:6**

Jesus said if we want to bear fruit, we must
remain in Him. The word *remain* simply means
staying somewhere continually.

Contrary to what many people think, you
cannot live from Sunday to Sunday without
spiritual food. You can't spend time with the Lord
once a week at church, ignore Him the rest of the
time, and still expect Him to be Lord of all you're
doing. John 15:6 makes that clear.

The moment a branch is broken off the vine,
it begins to die. It doesn't matter how close they
are to one another. You can lay that branch
beside the vine, but if they're not connected,
there will be no life flow of sap traveling from the
vine into the branch.

The same is true for us. When we get too busy to spend time with God in prayer and in His Word, when we get preoccupied with everyday things and disconnect from spending time with Him, we immediately begin to wither. We begin to lose spiritual energy when we aren't living in close contact with the Lord. Even though we still belong to Him and have His life within us, His energy is not flowing through us so we can't produce anything.

Suddenly, even when we know the right thing to do, we find ourselves lacking the power to do it. We need strength to bear fruit!

On the other hand, when you do remain in the Vine, you're sure to bear fruit. It has to happen! The Holy Spirit's power flowing through you will just naturally make what God has placed within you come out, and you will begin to act like the loving, joyful, peaceful, patient, kind, good, faithful, gentle, and self-controlled person you really are! You will overflow with His fruit!

backup
John 15:1-8

voice activate
I remain in Jesus and I overflow

with His fruit! John 15:5

Kenneth

Hit It From the Source

> "Jesus said to it [the fig tree], 'Let no one eat fruit from you ever again.' And His disciples heard it.... Now in the morning, as they passed by, they saw the fig tree dried up from the roots."
>
> —Mark 11:14,20, NKJV

You can't wipe out a weed simply by mowing it down. If you want to get rid of a weed, you must destroy its roots.

Did you know that's true in every other area of life? If you want to change a situation permanently, you must tackle it at its root. You can lose hundreds of pounds, for example, and you'll regain every one of them (and probably more) if you don't solve that weight problem at the root.

That is what's so awesomely powerful about faith. If it's founded on a promise from God to you, it will change things in your life from the roots up.

Read Mark 11 and you'll see what I mean. Jesus was walking from Bethany to Jerusalem with His disciples. He was hungry, but when He saw a fig tree that didn't have any figs, He "said to it, 'Let no one eat fruit from you ever again.' And his disciples heard it" (verse 14).

Jesus answered the fig tree because it spoke to Him first! By the very fact that it had no fruit, that tree was saying to Jesus, "Forget it, buddy. You aren't getting anything to eat here."

Your circumstances talk to you in the same way. Do you realize that? If you're standing against sickness, that sickness is talking to you. When you get up in the morning, it says, *You haven't received your healing. You're hurting all over. This faith stuff isn't working. You might as well go back to bed.*

Your situations will talk to you all the time. So do what Jesus did. Answer them! Get to the root. Say, "By His wounds I was healed! I am more than a conqueror in Christ Jesus!"

Speaking words in faith like that will change things. Jesus took on the fig tree at its root...and it made a permanent change. You have the same power. If you'll release your faith, you can hit even the most stubborn problem and dry it up at the source. You can get rid of it from the roots up!

b a c k u p
2 Corinthians 4:13-18

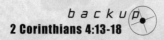

v o i c e   a c t i v a t e

I have the same spirit of faith as

Jesus. I believe and therefore I

speak. 2 Corinthians 4:13

The Zero Hour

**"As God's chosen people, holy and
dearly loved, clothe yourselves
with...patience."**
—Colossians 3:12

The most critical time when you're believing
God for something is after you pray...but before
you actually see the answer.

This is the critical time when things are
being set in motion by your faith, even though
you can't see anything. It's the time when
you're the most tempted to say, "Nothing is
happening. I prayed and believed, but I don't
have it. It looks like I never will. I guess I just
don't have enough faith."

You may want to say that—but don't! The
Bible says that every believer has received "the
measure of faith" (Romans 12:3). You don't need
more faith. What you need is something to
strengthen and undergird the faith you have, so it

will continue working until the answer comes. What you need is patience.

Patience is one of the characteristics God placed inside you when you became a Christian. It doesn't give in to tough times. It doesn't quit believing. Patience undergirds faith to keep it stable and strong when circumstances say, "It's impossible!"

Patience is the opposite of hopelessness. Ephesians 2:12 says that people who are not Christians are "without hope" and are "without God in the world."

We are not in the world without a Savior. We have "the hope held out in the gospel" (Colossians 1:23), and patience is associated with hope. Patience, you see, will hold on. It knows, "I have a promise from God, and I will stand. I will endure until the answer comes."

The force of patience is so powerful that it cannot be overcome. If you'll exercise the patience inside you, it will be there when you need it to help you stand. It will undergird your faith to keep you believing until the answer comes.

So, the next time you're tempted to say, "It's not working," give way to the force of patience instead. Faith and patience working together will make you a winner...and help you through the critical times!

backup
Psalm 128

voice activate
Because I have God, I am not without hope. My hope is in the gospel. I will be patient and endure until my answers come. Ephesians 2:12; Colossians 1:23

Kenneth **DAY 14**

Faith Is Not a Fad

> "Until we all reach unity in the faith and in the knowledge of the Son of God and become mature, attaining to the whole measure of the fullness of Christ."
> —Ephesians 4:13

Living the faith life for more than 30 years, I've become convinced that faith is not just a fad. It's much more than that.

God is moving. He is calling people from all denominations to move into a life of power. He is showing us a way to live successfully—day in and day out, in good times and bad times. Isn't that what we want? Isn't that what we need?

He is teaching us that faith in His Word works, even when nothing else does. He is calling us to live by faith, not just temporarily, but as Ephesians 4:13 says, "until we all reach unity in the faith and in the knowledge of the Son of God and become mature, attaining to the whole measure of the fullness of Christ."

If God is calling you to live a life of faith, and you've been tiptoeing around it...wondering if it's real or not...jump in now! Faith is not a fad. Faith is how God operates and lives...it's how He wants you to live.

Faith will open the door to success for you, and it will keep you there—safe and healed and wealthy in all areas of life. It will keep you armed and dangerous to Satan. It will keep you free from sin and enable you to grow into a man or woman of character. Faith will enable you to please God. Faith is a permanent way of life, and it's here to stay.

backup
Colossians 2:6-7

voice activate
I develop and attain oneness in faith with other believers. I am perfect and complete in Christ.

Ephesians 4:13, AMP

Gloria

Keep It Simple

> "The ones sown among the thorns are others who hear the Word; Then the cares and anxieties of the world and distractions of the age, and the pleasure and delight and false glamour and deceitfulness of riches, and the craving and passionate desire for other things creep in and choke and suffocate the Word, and it becomes fruitless."
>
> —Mark 4:18-19, AMP

Over the years, I've noticed how easy it is to get caught up in day-to-day living. In fact, it sometimes seems as though this world is like an octopus, always trying to grab you with its tentacles. If you don't watch out, it will wrap itself around you until you're completely tied up in the trivial things of this world.

Those trivial pursuits can hold you down and keep you from soaring on into the things of God. They can choke the Word out of your heart and leave you without faith and without power. That's what Mark 4:18-19 is talking about.

Here in America, we must be especially alert, because we have so many material possessions! We can easily spend all our time taking care of them.

As the Lord told a friend of mine in prayer one day, this nation has become a nation of maintenance men. We maintain our houses. We maintain our cars. We maintain our hair, our nails, and our clothes. The problem is, by the time we've done what it takes to maintain all the "things" in our lives, we often don't have any time left to maintain our spirit.

There's only one thing to do: Simplify your life.

There's nothing more important than spending time with God. So make whatever adjustments you must to spend time with Him. Whenever you take on anything new, count the cost—not just in money, but in time. Ask yourself, Can I afford this spiritually? Can I spare the precious hours and minutes this activity or thing will require and still have plenty of time to spend with the Lord?

If the answer is no, then set that thing aside. I realize that may mean passing up some things you enjoy. Remember, your aim is not to please yourself. It's to please God. Believe me, when you make sacrifices for Him, He always makes sure you're well-rewarded. Now, that's "the good life."

backup
Luke 12:22-31

voice activate

I throw off everything

that hinders and easily

entangles me. Hebrews 12:1

DAY 16

Eternal Health

> "I call heaven and earth to record this day against you, that I have set before you life and death, blessing and cursing: therefore choose life, that both thou and thy seed may live."
>
> —Deuteronomy 30:19, KJV

Tradition has taught that God uses sicknesses, trials, and tribulation to teach us. This idea, however, is not based on the Bible. God has never used sickness to discipline His children and keep them in line. Sickness is of Satan, and God doesn't need Satan to straighten us out!

"Kenneth, I see Christians that are sick all of the time. Why does God allow it?"

God allows it because we do. Why? Because He's given us the right to make our own choices, along with authority over the kingdom of darkness.

According to Deuteronomy 30:19, He has put life and death before us. Then He instructed us to choose life. It's up to us to make the decision.

You have the power to live after God's ways and resist sickness, or not to. You have the choice to let Satan run over you, or use the authority you have been given. Good gifts come from God. No matter what tradition has taught, sickness and disease simply don't fall into the category of good gifts—ever.

So make a decision today. Resist Satan's sicknesses and diseases. Give way to life!

b a c k u p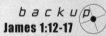
James 1:12-17

v o i c e   a c t i v a t e
God has set before me life and

death, blessings and curses. I

choose life! Deuteronomy 30:19

Get Aggressive!

> **"If you are willing and obedient, you shall eat the good of the land."**
> —Isaiah 1:19, AMP

God has always promised that if you are willing and obedient, you will "eat the good of the land." Being willing means more than just saying, "Well, Lord, if You want me to do well, I will." Being willing means that you determine to receive by faith what God has promised, no matter how things look.

That's what Ken and I had to do. When we saw in the Bible that wealth belonged to us, we were so deep in debt it looked like we would never get out, but we became willing anyway. We said, "In Jesus' Name, we will do well. We won't live in poverty. We receive all God has provided for us now!"

For years, I didn't understand that we needed to make a stand like that, so without realizing it, I allowed Satan to come in and give me a hard time over finances. Then one day, God showed me that I needed to use the same kind of stand for finances as for healing.

I had already learned to be aggressive about healing. Once Ken and I found out that Jesus took away our sickness, we refused to put up with it. We realized sickness was our enemy and we stood against it. We'd tell it, "No! God has rescued us from sickness. So don't come near us!"

One day God said to me, *Why don't you treat poverty the same way? Why do you put up with it? You say you've been rescued from it, but you haven't resisted it like you do sickness and disease.*

When I heard that, I determined to make a change. I began to aggressively resist poverty the same way I resisted sickness, and it made a big difference!

I must warn you though, it wasn't easy. It takes effort and determination to resist it. If you want to do well financially now or in the future, you'll need to keep God's promises in your heart.

You'll need to think about what God says all the time. You'll need to get aggressive!

backup
Galatians 3:13-14

voice activate
I am willing and obedient.

I always eat the best from

the land. Isaiah 1:19

Kenneth   **DAY 18**

Power in Praise

> "O Lord, our Lord, how majestic is your
> name in all the earth! You have set your
> glory above the heavens. From the lips of
> children and infants you have ordained
> praise because of your enemies, to
> silence the foe and the avenger."
> —Psalm 8:1-2

When you've prayed and believed God to
change circumstances, then you should praise and
thank Him in the middle of those circumstances
while you wait for them to change.

There's power in praise. If you praise God,
you'll be able to triumph over every attack. Psalm
8:1-2 confirms that. Satan is not going to hang
around listening to you praise God. Praise shuts
his mouth. So put it to work.

Praise God that the trouble is gone even while
it's still there. Praise Him for setting you free.

Praise Him for the blood of Jesus that paid the
price for your sin and rescued you from every curse.

Praise Him in the morning. Shout your way to work every day.

Praise Him at noon.

Shout your way home every afternoon.

Praise Him at night.

Praise Him when you don't feel like praising Him! It will make a difference.

Gloria and I have applied truths like this for more than 30 years, and God has brought us out on top every time. He'll do the same for you!

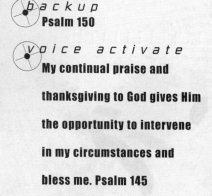

backup
Psalm 150

voice activate
My continual praise and thanksgiving to God gives Him the opportunity to intervene in my circumstances and bless me. Psalm 145

Gloria

He Wants Your Heart

> "Honor the Lord with your wealth, with the firstfruits of all your crops; then your barns will be filled to overflowing, and your vats will brim over with new wine."
>
> —Proverbs 3:9-10

Have you ever wanted God to bless you? Well, sure you have! God has already given us more than we ever dreamed possible. He has rescued us from darkness. He has provided healing for us. He has blessed us in a thousand different ways. That's what we should remember every time we tithe. We should give with a thankful attitude.

If you'll read Deuteronomy 26, you'll see that's what God instructed the Israelites to do. He didn't want them to simply toss their tithe into the offering plate. He wanted their hearts in what they were doing. He wants the same from us.

When we give our tithe, we should worship God and say, "Father, once I was lost, a prisoner of sin with no hope, but You sent Jesus to rescue me. You sent Him to die so I could live. Thank You, Lord, for rescuing me from the darkness and bringing me into the Light. Thank You for receiving my tithe as an act of my worship to You."

Don't stop there! Just like the Israelites, say, "Lord, here's my tithe. I haven't kept it for myself. I've given it just as You commanded. So look down from heaven and bless me!" (Deuteronomy 26:13-15).

Does that kind of talk make you nervous? Do you think God will be offended if you tell Him to bless you? He won't! He'll be delighted. After all, it's His idea to bless us in the first place! It's what He's wanted to do all along.

So don't be shy. Tithe boldly! Tithe gladly! Give God 10 percent of what you make, and give Him 100 percent of your heart. Then shout, "The Lord be exalted, who delights in the well-being of his servant!" (Psalm 35:27).

backup
Deuteronomy 26

voice activate

I honor the Lord with my

wealth, with the firstfruits

of all my increase. My barns

are filled to overflowing

and my vats brim over with

new wine. Proverbs 3:9-10

Kenneth

You Are Anointed

> "You hold a sacred appointment, you
> have been given an unction—you have
> been anointed by the Holy One."
> —1 John 2:20, AMP

We've thrown around the word *anointing* in churches for years without really understanding what it means. If we're to walk in God's power, it has to become real to us.

The anointing is God's presence—who He is. It's the thing that makes God God. The anointing is God on you enabling you to do things that are impossible for you to do alone.

For instance, you can't heal anyone. Even Jesus as a physical man couldn't heal anyone. His physical being came from Mary. He was as human as she was. Yet His perfect, sinless being—speaking God's promises—caused God's Anointing to come on Him without measure (see John 3:34, KJV).

It's not hard for our minds to understand that God's Anointing was on Jesus. What's tough to comprehend is that the same anointing can be on us.

"No way! I'm not sinless."

No, but as far as God is concerned you are. That's what grace is all about—giving us the anointing when we don't deserve it!

Just like Jesus couldn't heal in His own humanness, neither can you. With the anointing, Jesus brought healing, and so can you. Everything you need to do today can be done in the Anointed One and His Anointing.

His Anointing is on you, in you, and all over you. Because of it, you can do things you couldn't normally do...whether it's day-to-day responsibilities, or placing your hands on someone and zapping them with the healing power of God. You can be and do everything God created you to be and do in His Anointing. You are anointed!

backup
Acts 8:5-8

voice activate
I am anointed and I know

the truth. 1 John 2:20

Gloria

Success Is Hunting You

"The blessing of the Lord brings wealth, and he adds no trouble to it."
—Proverbs 10:22

How much do you want to succeed in life? Enough to change what you're saying? Enough to change where your attention is focused? Enough to act on God's Word even when the rest of the world is telling you it will never work?

If you want it that much, the Bible guarantees you'll get it.

I must warn you, though. Satan won't like it. He'll try to talk you out of it, and since he knows God's success formula, he knows exactly what tactics to use.

He'll pressure you to say negative things. He'll try to distract you from the Word and get your attention on anything—it doesn't matter what it is, as long as it isn't the Word.

His goal is to stop your faith. He knows it's the only force that can cause impossible situations to change. He also knows that it comes from God's Word. So when he sees that Word going in your heart and hears you speaking it, he doesn't just sit there. He starts talking. Doubtful thoughts will come into your mind, thoughts that are just the opposite of what God has said.

It is important to remember that those thoughts don't become yours unless you believe them and speak them. That's what he wants you to do, of course. If the Bible says you're healed, he'll tell you you're sick. If the Bible says you're forgiven, he'll say you're still guilty. If the Bible says your needs are met, he'll tell you they're not.

However, if you hold on to your faith, and keep the Word in your mouth and in your heart, you can't lose. There's no force Satan can bring against you that is stronger than God's Word. It will make you a winner every time.

So if you've been wanting true success and it's been eluding you, quit wondering if you have what it takes to make it—and remember instead Who is with you and in you. Then turn to the Bible and put God's success formula to work in your life. Soon, you won't be hunting for success...it will be hunting you!

backup
Romans 8:31-34

voice activate
The blessing of the Lord brings me wealth, and He adds no trouble to it. Proverbs 10:22

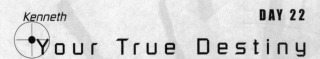

Kenneth   **DAY 22**

Your True Destiny

"Put on the full armor of God."
—Ephesians 6:11

Did you know that right here, in the middle of the same storms that are tearing the world apart, you and I and every other Christian can win in life?

We can put on the full armor of God, walk right into the middle of the worst circumstances the world has to throw at us, and none of them will be able to bring us down.

That's why God told us to put on His armor in the first place! He knew it would protect us. The Word of God and the full armor of God is bulletproof. It's sickness-proof, debt-proof, depression-proof. With it, you'll stand when everything around you is falling apart—but you have to get dressed!

You can't just give God's Word a passing nod and then go on watching what the world watches and saying what the world says. If you keep copying the world's ways, you're going to share in the world's destiny. But if you'll copy Jesus, you'll share His destiny. It's your choice.

Romans 12:2 says, "Do not conform any longer to the pattern of this world, but be transformed by the renewing of your mind. Then you will be able to test and approve what God's will is—his good, pleasing and perfect will."

You won't find God's will for your life by copying the world. You'll find it by copying Jesus. "If you hold to my teaching, you are really my disciples. Then you will know the truth, and the truth will set you free" (John 8:31).

So put on the full armor and stand strong. Being a winner is your true destiny!

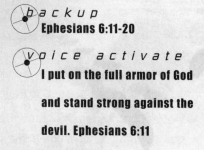

b a c k u p
Ephesians 6:11-20

v o i c e   a c t i v a t e
I put on the full armor of God and stand strong against the devil. Ephesians 6:11

Gloria   **DAY 23**

Back to Basics

> "Therefore, since we are surrounded by
> such a great cloud of witnesses, let us
> throw off everything that hinders and
> the sin that so easily entangles, and let
> us run with perseverance the race
> marked out for us."
>
> —Hebrews 12:1

Several years ago, our ministry went into
debt—we were behind by nearly $6 million in
bills! It didn't look like there were any easy
answers. We thought about selling everything
so we could pay off the deficit. Then, we
wouldn't have had any place to house the
ministry operations.

Things looked dark, but do you know what
got us through that situation? It wasn't some
new insight from God. It wasn't some flash from
heaven bringing us an instant solution.

What overcame that debt was the same
thing that put food on our table more than thirty

years ago when we first began to live by faith: patiently putting God's Word into practice.

We began listening to teachings from people who really ministered to us. We went back to basics—learning about the words we say and how to use our faith. Where we discovered we'd slipped, we corrected ourselves. We put God's Word in our hearts and spoke out His promises.

In other words, we did what James 1:4 says. We let that trial work patience in us, and when it was done, we had everything we needed. What's more, others saw how God helped us through, and it has shown them the way, too.

That's the risk Satan always takes when he puts you through a trial. He takes the chance you'll come through stronger than you were before, instead of weaker. He takes the chance of you becoming a living example of God's power.

If you're facing a challenging situation, and Satan is up to risky business, just put into practice the basic truths you've already learned. Do what you know to do, and God will take care of the rest.

backup
James 1:1-8

voice activate
I throw off everything that

hinders and the sin that so

easily entangles me. I run with

perseverance the race marked

out for me. Hebrews 12:1

You're in Charge

> "You made him [man] ruler over the
> works of your hands; you put everything
> under his feet."
> —Psalm 8:6

"Well, friend, you have to remember...God is sovereign."

You've probably heard someone say that at some time, usually in religious-sounding tones, when circumstances seem to fall short of what God has promised they would be.

As spiritual as that phrase might sound, it really bothers me. It's not that I don't believe God is sovereign. Certainly He is. According to *Webster's Dictionary, sovereign* means "above or superior to all others; supreme in power, rank or authority." Without question, God is all those things.

All too often, when people refer to God being sovereign, what they're actually saying is, "You never know what God will do. After all,

He's all-powerful and He does whatever He wants whenever He wants."

The problem with that is that it releases us of all responsibility. After all, if that's the case, God will do what He wants anyway, so we might as well kick back and watch professional wrestling for the rest of our lives and forget about everything, right?

Wrong. After more than 30 years of studying the Bible and preaching, I've come to realize that God does very few things—if anything—in this earth without man's cooperation. Even though it belongs to God...it is His creation and He owns it.

According to Psalm 8:6, God Himself put mankind in charge. He doesn't intervene just whenever He wants. He respects the place He has given us. So, until man's time on this planet ends, God restricts His power, taking action only when He is asked to do so.

Since the people who do the asking are often very quiet people who do their praying in secret, it may appear at times that God simply acts on His own. The Bible teaches that God's connection with man is a prayer and faith connection. When you see Him act in a mighty way, you can be sure there was someone somewhere praying to bring Him on the scene.

backup
James 5:13-18

voice activate
God has made me the ruler over all the works of His hands. He has put everything under my feet. Psalm 8:6

Gloria

DAY 25

A Word to the Wise

"Everyone who hears these words of mine and puts them into practice is like a wise man who built his house on the rock. The rain came down, the streams rose, and the winds blew and beat against that house; yet it did not fall, because it had its foundation on the rock."

—Matthew 7:24-25

I've been telling people to spend time in the Word for years now. Almost everywhere I preach, no matter what topic I'm talking about, it seems I always get back to the importance of putting God's Word first.

You may have heard me say it a hundred times, but hearing it isn't enough. It's doing it that will make you successful.

Jesus taught us that principle in Matthew 7. There He told about two men. Both of them heard the Word, yet Jesus said one of the men was foolish and the other wise. What was the difference between the two? The wise man acted on what he heard and the foolish man didn't.

You may know full well that you need to spend time reading your Bible, but unless you act on what you know, it won't do you any good when the storms of life come.

So take action! Start setting aside time to read your Bible each day. Begin making it the number one priority on your schedule. Don't wait until you're faced with some terrible, stormy situation.

Have you ever tried to build a house in a storm? Ken has been through several hurricanes. He has seen the wind blow so hard that coconuts shot through the air like cannonballs. Just think about some poor fellow out there trying to build his house with the wind blowing 120 mph!

Don't do that. Don't wait until you're desperate to make time for studying God's Word. Make the decision and start today.

Then, when the storms of life come against your house, you'll be totally cool, calm, and collected. You'll be glad that you didn't let Satan talk you into being too busy for the Word.

b a c k u p
Proverbs 1:1-9

v o i c e a c t i v a t e
I am wise because I hear God's

Words and I put them into

practice. Matthew 7:24

What Are You Becoming?

"From the fruit of his mouth a man's stomach is filled; with the harvest from his lips he is satisfied. The tongue has the power of life and death, and those who love it will eat its fruit."

—Proverbs 18:20-21

If you're not sure what you're becoming, let me give you a hint. You're going to be whatever you think about and talk about all the time.

I can listen to you talk for thirty minutes and tell you exactly what you'll become. It doesn't take a prophet to do that. It just takes someone who will listen to your words.

So listen to yourself. If you don't like what you hear, change it. Become something better by beginning to think God's Word, talk God's Word, and act on God's Word.

Nobody on earth can determine what you're going to become but you. Yes, you! Don't blame it on Satan. He can't change it. Don't blame it on your parents, your background, or your circumstances, and certainly, don't blame God.

Forget your past...and do what Abraham did. The Bible says, "He did not consider his own body, already dead (since he was about a hundred years old), and the deadness of Sarah's womb" (Romans 4:19, NKJV).

He just said to himself, *Old man, you don't count. Neither do you, Granny. What counts is God's promise, and I am exactly what God says I am.*

Do you want to become what God says you are? Do you want to be wise? Do you want to be bold? Do you want to be a powerful witness to your friends and coworkers? What is your dream?

You can determine your outcome in life by changing your words to match God's words and releasing your faith. You can become all you were meant to be.

backup
Matthew 12:33-37

voice activate
My stomach is filled from the

fruit of my mouth, and with the

harvest of my lips, I am satisfied.

Proverbs 18:20

Gloria

The Path to Promotion

> "Servants, obey in everything those who
> are your earthly masters, not only when
> their eyes are on you, as pleasers of
> men, but in simplicity of purpose (with
> all your heart) because of your
> reverence for the Lord and as a sincere
> expression of your devotion to Him."
>
> —Colossians 3:22, AMP

You may not realize it, but if you're a Christian,
you have a quality within you that is in great
demand in the world today. It's a quality
employers prize so highly that they'll promote
people who have it—and often pay top dollar for it.

What is this precious quality? The quality
of faithfulness.

Employers are desperate for faithful people.
The world is full of employees who will do just
enough to keep from getting fired. It's a treasure
for employers to find a person who works

wholeheartedly at his job, who is trustworthy and dependable and honest. So when an employer finds a person like that, he's usually eager to promote him.

The fact is, every Christian ought to be that kind of person. Each of us should live a lifestyle of faithfulness. As Ken says, in every situation we should do what's right, do it because it's right, and do it right.

We should follow Colossians 3:22-24. It's God's instruction for employees. Ken and I have seen some of the staff members in our ministry take that attitude and, as a result, be promoted time and again. One man started out with the job of duplicating tapes for us, but over the years he was so faithful that he eventually became the director over the business affairs of the entire ministry.

You may think, *Well, I don't know if that'll work for me. After all, the world is full of unfair bosses. What if mine won't reward my faithfulness?*

That's no problem. The Scripture doesn't say your reward will come from your employer. It says your reward will come from the Lord!

So make up your mind to put your whole heart into your work, no matter how menial or unpleasant it may seem to be. Do it well. Do it with a smile and enthusiasm. Soon, you will receive a promotion in return...even if that promotion means a different but better job!

backup
Galatians 6:7-10

voice activate
I obey my earthly masters in

everything with sincerity of

heart and reverence for

the Lord. Colossians 3:22

Make That Decision⊕

> "[I will] not in any degree leave you
> helpless, nor forsake nor let [you] down!"
> —**Hebrews 13:5,** AMP

If God has called you to do something,
something that you think is impossible, chances
are Satan has been bombarding you with
thoughts of doubt, fear, and discouragement.

Don't let him lead you down that road. Don't
let him keep you from remembering that God has
the ability and faithfulness to get the job done.
Resist the temptation to think about your problems
and inability—resist the temptation to worry.

Stop struggling and start resting. Relax. God
knows that what He has called you to do is
impossible. He knows you are having a problem
with that fact. He doesn't mind waiting while you
draw on His promises and develop the courage
you need for the task.

You don't have to panic. Just keep
reminding yourself that as long as you have

your Bible and your faith, you can do anything God tells you to do.

Put thoughts about your own weaknesses behind you and focus instead on God's awesome ability. Start saying to yourself, *God is with me! He will not, He will not, HE WILL NOT leave me helpless, forget me, or let me down!*

Then open your Bible and choose to believe what it says about you. Treat it as God's blood-sworn oath to you. Keep it in front of your eyes. Keep it in your ears. Keep it coming out of your mouth. Make a rock-solid decision to stick with it until the strength of God Himself rises up within you and overwhelms the fear.

Once you make that decision, there's no turning back. It's on to bigger and better things!

b a c k u p
Philippians 4:4-9

v o i c e   a c t i v a t e
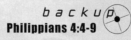
The Lord won't leave me helpless

at all. He won't forget me or

let me down. Hebrews 13:5

Center Your Life Around God

> "Love [God's love in us] does not insist
> on its own rights or its own way, for it is
> not self-seeking."
>
> —1 Corinthians 13:5, AMP

God loves the unlovely. No matter how bad,
mean, or ornery someone might be, if they'll turn
to Him, He'll cleanse them and forgive them.

That's the way God loves us, and that's the
way He expects us to love each other. In 1
Corinthians 13, He gives us a detailed description
of that kind of love. According to the Bible, it's
God's love that sets you apart. You and I have a
high calling. We're called to live a life of love just
like Jesus did.

We must die to our own selfish tendencies
and desires. We must stop centering our lives on
what we want and what we feel. We must stop
looking out for ourselves all the time. Walking in

love means we set aside our own rights and look out for the other person's instead.

That may sound tough, but it's actually the easiest way to be blessed—because when you walk in love, God takes care of you! The Bible says, "The eyes of the Lord run to and fro throughout the whole earth, to show Himself strong in behalf of those whose heart is blameless toward Him" (2 Chronicles 16:9, AMP). When you walk in love, blessings are coming your way!

Not only that, when you stop being selfish, you'll be a happier person. When you're self-centered, you're always thinking about yourself. You're always thinking about someone who did you wrong...or how much you have to do.

It's impossible for a selfish person to stay happy because everything centers around him. We're not made to live that way. We're not big enough or powerful enough for everything to center around us.

As a Christian, you've been rescued from selfishness. You don't have to center your life around yourself. You have the power to center your life around God instead. You can keep your mind on obeying His Word and living a life of love! He will take care of everything else (Matthew 6:33).

b a c k u p
Ephesians 4:1-3

v o i c e   a c t i v a t e
I walk in love. I seek God and His

ways, and He takes care of

everything else. Matthew 6:33

Kenneth   **DAY 30**

Get Beyond the Requirements!

> "Your attitude should be the same as that of Christ Jesus: Who, being in very nature God, did not consider equality with God something to be grasped, but made himself nothing, taking the very nature of a servant, being made in human likeness."
>
> —Philippians 2:5-7

More than any other man, Paul knew what it was to be free. He was born a free Roman citizen. Then he made Jesus his Lord, and God showed him how he had been rescued from the rulership of darkness and brought into a new life in Jesus. Yet he bowed his knee to Jesus and said, "I give away my freedom. I give away my will. I give it all away to serve You. I'll live for You and I'll die for You."

Jesus Himself set the pattern for such servanthood when He was on earth, and Philippians 2:5-7 encourages us to follow His example.

As a servant, your attitude will be like Jesus' attitude: "Not my will, but yours be done" (Luke 22:42). You'll say, "I don't care what it takes; I will obey God. If He wants me to lock myself up in my closet and pray all weekend, that's what I'll do, because I'm His servant!"

Some people like to argue that God would never require such sacrifices from us.

That's just proof that those people aren't servants, because true servants aren't interested in doing only what God requires. True servants want to be totally committed to God and His Word. They want everything they do to be led by Him. As a result, God rewards them. He gives them His gifts. He gives them His power, and He uses them to do great things in His Name.

If you want God to give His gifts to you, if you want to do great things in His Name, then you'll first need to become a servant—one who goes beyond the requirements.

backup
Philippians 2:5-11

voice activate
Lord, not my will, but Yours be

done in my life. Luke 22:42

Hearing From Heaven

"The backsliding of the simple shall
slay them, and the careless ease of
[self-confident] fools shall destroy
them. But whoso hearkens to me
[Wisdom], shall dwell securely and in
confident trust, and shall be quiet
without fear or dread of evil."

—**Proverbs 1:32-33**, AMP

There is nothing—absolutely nothing!—on
this earth that's as valuable as God's wisdom. It
is the key to success, health, long life, peace,
and security. All of these are available to those
who learn from and live by His wisdom.

Oddly enough, many Christians don't seek
God's wisdom until their backs are against the
wall. They wait until trouble hits, and then, in
desperation, they listen hard for God's voice. All
too often they are unable to hear it.

Why? Because, as the voice of Wisdom says in Proverbs 1:24-28: "I have called and you refused [to answer],....you have treated as nothing all my counsel, and would accept none of my reproof, I also will laugh at your calamity; I will mock when the thing comes that shall cause you terror and panic, When your panic comes as a storm and desolation, and your calamity comes on as a whirlwind, when distress and anguish come upon you. Then they will call upon me [Wisdom], but I will not answer; they will seek me early and diligently, but they will not find me" (AMP).

Don't ever let yourself get caught in a situation like that. Don't ever let yourself get to the point where you're unable to hear from heaven.

Hearing from heaven is the most important thing in your whole life! That's because you can never come up with a problem too big for God to solve. The important thing to remember, however, is that you can't turn God's wisdom on and off like a water faucet. Hearing from heaven must be part of your lifestyle.

If you want to be sure that God's wisdom will be there for you when a crisis hits, you need to start listening for His guidance now. Learn to seek His wisdom, to listen for His instructions on the little, everyday matters of life. That way, when the big problems come, you'll be ready. You'll be in the habit of hearing from heaven.

b a c k u p
Proverbs 4:7-9

v o i c e   a c t i v a t e
Because I listen to God's

wisdom, I am secure and

confident, without fear or

dread. Proverbs 1:33

Prayer for Salvation and Baptism in the Holy Spirit

Heavenly Father, I come to You in the Name of Jesus. Your Word says, *"Whosoever shall call on the name of the Lord shall be saved"* (Acts 2:21, KJV). I am calling on You. I pray and ask Jesus to come into my heart and be Lord over my life according to Romans 10:9-10, KJV. *"If thou shalt confess with thy mouth the Lord Jesus, and shalt believe in thine heart that God hath raised him from the dead, thou shalt be saved. For with the heart man believeth unto righteousness; and with the mouth confession is made unto salvation."* I do that now. I confess that Jesus is Lord, and I believe in my heart that God raised Him from the dead.

I am now reborn! I am a Christian—a child of Almighty God! I am saved! You also said in Your Word, *"If ye then, being evil, know how to give good gifts unto your children: HOW MUCH MORE shall your heavenly Father give the Holy Spirit to them that ask him?"* (Luke 11:13, KJV). I'm also asking You to fill me with the Holy Spirit. Holy Spirit, rise up within me as I praise God. I fully expect to speak with other tongues as You give me the utterance (see Acts 2:4).

Begin to praise God for filling you with the Holy Spirit. Speak those words and syllables you receive—not in your own language, but the language given to you by the Holy Spirit. You have to use your own voice. God will not force you to speak. Worship and praise Him in your heavenly language—in other tongues.

Continue with the blessing God has given you and pray in tongues each day.

You are a born-again, Spirit-filled believer. You'll never be the same!

Find a good Word of God preaching church, and become a part of a church family who will love and care for you as you love and care for them.

We need to be connected to each other. It increases our strength in God. It's God's plan for us.

About the Authors

Kenneth and Gloria Copeland are the best-selling authors of more than 60 books such as the popular *Walk With God*, *Managing God's Mutual Funds*, and *God's Will for You*. Together they have co-authored numerous other books, including *Family Promises*. As founders of Kenneth Copeland Ministries in Fort Worth, Texas, Kenneth and Gloria are in their 33rd year of circling the globe with the uncompromised Word of God, preaching and teaching a lifestyle of victory for every Christian.

Their daily and Sunday *Believer's Voice of Victory* television broadcasts now air on more than 500 stations around the world, and their *Believer's Voice of Victory* and *Shout!* magazines are distributed to more than 1 million adults and children worldwide. Their international prison ministry reaches an average of 60,000 new inmates every year and receives more than 17,000 pieces of correspondence each month. Their teaching materials can also be found on the World Wide Web. With offices and staff in the United States, Canada, England, Australia, South Africa, and Ukraine, Kenneth and Gloria's teaching materials—books, magazines, tapes, and videos—have been translated into at least 22 languages to reach the world with the love of God.

Learn more about Kenneth Copeland Ministries by visiting our Web site at www.kcm.org.

Books Available From Kenneth Copeland Ministries

by Kenneth Copeland

* A Ceremony of Marriage
  A Matter of Choice
  Covenant of Blood
  Faith and Patience—The Power Twins
* Freedom From Fear
  Giving and Receiving
  Honor—Walking in Honesty, Truth and Integrity
  How to Conquer Strife
  How to Discipline Your Flesh
  How to Receive Communion
  Living at the End of Time—A Time of Supernatural Increase
  Love Never Fails
  Managing God's Mutual Funds
* Now Are We in Christ Jesus
* Our Covenant With God
  Partnership, Sharing the Vision—Sharing the Grace
* Prayer—Your Foundation for Success
* Prosperity: The Choice Is Yours
  Rumors of War
* Sensitivity of Heart
* Six Steps to Excellence in Ministry
* Sorrow Not! Winning Over Grief and Sorrow
* The Decision Is Yours
* The Force of Faith
* The Force of Righteousness
  The Image of God in You
  The Laws of Prosperity
* The Mercy of God
  The Miraculous Realm of God's Love
  The Outpouring of the Spirit—The Result of Prayer
* The Power of the Tongue
  The Power to Be Forever Free
  The Troublemaker
* The Winning Attitude
  Turn Your Hurts Into Harvests
* Welcome to the Family
* You Are Healed!
  Your Right-Standing With God

by Gloria Copeland

* And Jesus Healed Them All
  Are You Listening?
  Are You Ready?
  Be a Vessel of Honor
  Build Your Financial Foundation
  Fight On!
  Go With the Flow
  God's Prescription for Divine Health
  God's Success Formula
  God's Will for You
  God's Will for Your Healing
  God's Will Is Prosperity
* God's Will Is the Holy Spirit
  Grace That Makes Us Holy
* Harvest of Health
  Hearing From Heaven
  Hidden Treasures
  Living in Heaven's Blessings Now
* Love—The Secret to Your Success
  No Deposit—No Return
  Pleasing the Father

Pressing In—It's Worth It All
Shine On!
The Power to Live a New Life
The Unbeatable Spirit of Faith
To Know Him
Walk With God
Well Worth the Wait
Your Promise of Protection

Books Co-authored by Kenneth and Gloria Copeland

Family Promises
Healing Promises
Prosperity Promises
Protection Promises

* From Faith to Faith—A Daily Guide to Victory
From Faith to Faith—A Perpetual Calendar

Load Up Devotional
Load Up for Graduates

One Word From God Can Change Your Life
  One Word From God Series
  • One Word From God Can Change Your Destiny
  • One Word From God Can Change Your Family
  • One Word From God Can Change Your Finances
  • One Word From God Can Change Your Formula for Success
  • One Word From God Can Change Your Health
  • One Word From God Can Change Your Nation
  • One Word From God Can Change Your Prayer Life
  • One Word From God Can Change Your Relationships

  Over The Edge—A Youth Devotional

Pursuit of His Presence—A Daily Devotional
Pursuit of His Presence—A Perpetual Calendar

Other Books Published by KCP

The First 30 Years—A Journey of Faith
    The story of the lives of Kenneth and Gloria Copeland.
Real People. Real Needs. Real Victories.
    A book of testimonies to encourage your faith.

John G. Lake—His Life, His Sermons, His Boldness of Faith
The Holiest of All by Andrew Murray
The New Testament in Modern Speech by Richard Francis Weymouth

Products Designed for Today's Children and Youth

Baby Praise Board Book
Baby Praise Christmas Board Book
Noah's Ark Coloring Book
The Best of Shout! Adventure Comics
The Shout! Joke Book
The Shout! Super-Activity Book

*Commander Kellie and the Superkids*_{SM} Books:
The SWORD Adventure Book
Commander Kellie and the Superkids_{SM} Series

    Middle Grade Novels by Christopher P.N. Maselli

    #1 The Mysterious Presence
    #2 The Quest for the Second Half
    #3 Escape From Jungle Island
    #4 In Pursuit of the Enemy
    #5 Caged Rivalry
    #6 Mystery of the Missing Junk
The SWORD Adventure Book

*Available in Spanish

World Offices of
Kenneth Copeland Ministries

For more information about KCM and a free catalog,
please write the office nearest you:

Kenneth Copeland Ministries
Fort Worth, Texas 76192-0001

Kenneth Copeland
Locked Bag 2600
Mansfield Delivery Centre
QUEENSLAND 4122
AUSTRALIA

Kenneth Copeland
Post Office Box 15
BATH
BA1 3XN
ENGLAND U.K.

Kenneth Copeland
Private Bag X 909
FONTAINEBLEAU
2032
REPUBLIC OF SOUTH AFRICA

Kenneth Copeland
Post Office Box 378
Surrey, B.C.
V3T 5B6
CANADA

UKRAINE
L'VIV 290000
Post Office Box 84
Kenneth Copeland Ministries
L'VIV 290000
UKRAINE

We're Here for You!

BELIEVER'S VOICE OF VICTORY TELEVISION BROADCAST

Join Kenneth and Gloria Copeland and the *Believer's Voice of Victory* broadcasts Monday through Friday and on Sunday each week,* and learn how faith in God's Word can take your life from ordinary to extraordinary. This teaching from God's Word is designed to get you where you want to be—on top!

You can catch the *Believer's Voice of Victory* broadcast on your local cable or satellite channels.

*Check your local listings for times and stations in your area.

BELIEVER'S VOICE OF VICTORY MAGAZINE

Enjoy inspired teaching and encouragement from Kenneth and Gloria Copeland and guest ministers each month in the Believer's Voice of Victory magazine. Also included are real-life testimonies of God's miraculous power and divine intervention into the lives of people just like you!

It's more than just a magazine, it's a ministry.

SHOUT! ...THE DYNAMIC MAGAZINE JUST FOR KIDS!

Shout! The Voice of Victory for Kids is a Bible-charged, action-packed, bimonthly magazine available FREE to kids everywhere! Featuring Wichita Slim and Commander Kellie and the Superkids, *Shout!* is filled with colorful adventure comics, challenging games and puzzles, exciting short stories, solve-it-yourself mysteries, and much more!

Stand up, sign up, and get ready to Shout!

To receive a FREE subscription to *Believer's Voice of Victory*, or to give a child you know a FREE subscription to *Shout!*, write:

Kenneth Copeland Ministries
Fort Worth, Texas 76192-0001
Or call: 1-800-600-7395
(9 a.m.-5 p.m. CT)

Or visit our Web site at:
www.kcm.org

If you are writing from outside the U.S., please contact the KCM office nearest you. Addresses for all Kenneth Copeland Ministries offices are listed on the preceding page.

www.harrisonhouse.com

Fast. Easy. Convenient!

- ◆ New Book Information
- ◆ Look Inside the Book
- ◆ Press Releases
- ◆ Bestsellers

- ◆ Free E-News
- ◆ Author Biographies
- ◆ Upcoming Books
- ◆ Share Your Testimony

For the latest in book news and author information, please visit us on the Web at www.harrisonhouse.com. Get up-to-date pictures and details on all our powerful and life-changing products. Sign up for our e-mail newsletter, *Friends of the House,* and receive free monthly information on our authors and products including testimonials, author announcements, and more!

Harrison House—
Books That Bring Hope, Books That Bring Change

The Harrison House Vision

Proclaiming the truth and the power
Of the Gospel of Jesus Christ
With excellence;

Challenging Christians to
Live victoriously,
Grow spiritually,
Know God intimately.